Catfish Clues
What Is a Fish?

By LINDA AYERS

Illustrated by NICOLA O'BYRNE

Music Arranged and Produced by DREW TEMPERANTE

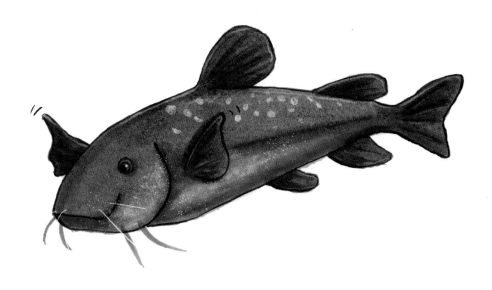

CANTATA
LEARNING

WWW.CANTATALEARNING.COM

CANTATA
LEARNING

Published by Cantata Learning
1710 Roe Crest Drive
North Mankato, MN 56003
www.cantatalearning.com

A note to educators and librarians from the publisher: Cantata Learning has provided the following data to assist in book processing and suggested use of Cantata Learning product.

Publisher's Cataloging-in-Publication Data
Prepared by Librarian Consultant: Ann-Marie Begnaud
Library of Congress Control Number: 2015958222
    Catfish Clues : What Is a Fish?
    Series: Animal World : Animal Kingdom Boogie
    By Linda Ayers
    Illustrated by Nicola O'Byrne
    Summary: Discover the characteristics of catfish and other fish in this fun song paired with beautiful illustrations.
    ISBN: 978-1-63290-584-0 (library binding/CD)
    ISBN: 978-1-63290-566-6 (paperback/CD)
Suggested Dewey and Subject Headings:
    Dewey: E 597
    LCSH Subject Headings: Fishes – Anatomy – Juvenile literature. | Fishes – Behavior – Juvenile literature. | Fishes – Songs and music – Texts. | Fishes – Juvenile sound recordings.
    Sears Subject Headings: Fishes. | Aquatic animals. | School songbooks. | Children's songs. | Popular music.
    BISAC Subject Headings: JUVENILE NONFICTION / Animals / Fishes. | JUVENILE NONFICTION / Music / Songbooks. | JUVENILE NONFICTION / Science & Nature / Zoology.

Book design and art direction, Tim Palin Creative
Editorial direction, Flat Sole Studio
Music direction, Elizabeth Draper
Music arranged and produced by Drew Temperante

Printed in the United States of America in North Mankato, Minnesota.
072016   0335CGF16

ACCESS THE MUSIC!

SCAN CODE WITH MOBILE APP

CANTATALEARNING.COM

What is a fish? Sharks, guppies, clownfish, and catfish are types of fish. They are all animals that live underwater and breath through **gills**. But not all fish look alike. Sharks are big, guppies are small, and clownfish are very colorful. Then there are catfish. They have **whiskers** and do not have scales like other fish.

To learn more about fish, turn the page and sing along!

Catfish knew that he was different.
The other fish called him names.
He was big, and he had whiskers,
and his skin was not the same.

Schools of fish all swim together.
They all look the same.
With no teachers, math, or recess,
safety in numbers is their game.

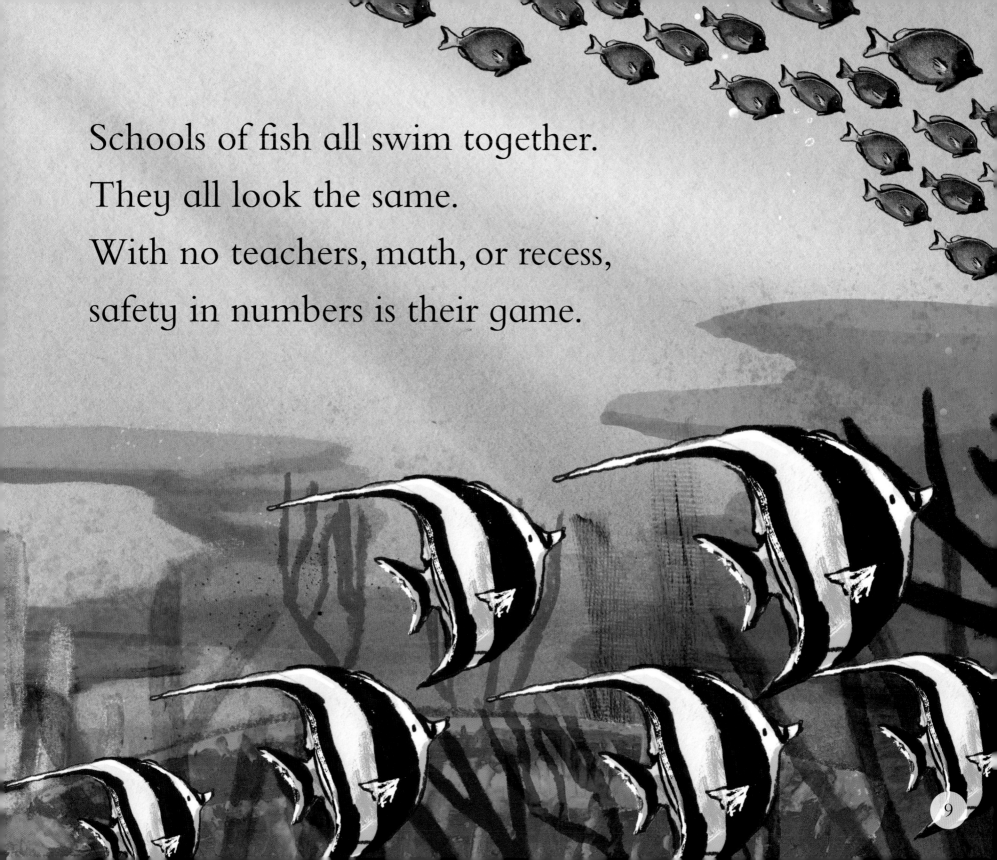

Is that a fish? How can you tell?

Does it live in water and have scales?

Do a tail and fins help it to swim?

Do gills let it breathe **oxygen**?

10

Yes! That's a fish!

11

Some fish live in salty water,
oceans where they swim free.
Others live in rivers, lakes, and ponds,
or **aquariums** for us to see.

Fish eat what's in the water,
wherever they may live,
plants or insects, worms or frogs,
fish or shrimp, or **pollywogs**.

Is that a fish? How can you tell?

Does it live in water and have scales?

Do a tail and fins help it to swim?

Do gills let it breathe oxygen?

Yes! That's a fish!

Can you wiggle your tail?

Can you splash your fins?

Can you swim in the water?

Do it all again!

Can you wiggle your tail?
Can you splash your fins?

Can you swim in the water
with your fishy friends?

17

Catfish was a different fish.
He was happy without scales,
but just like his friends, he had fishy parts
like gills and fins and a tail.

Is that a fish? How can you tell?

Does it live in water and have scales?

Do a tail and fins help it to swim?

Do gills let it breathe oxygen?

Yes! That's a fish!

SONG LYRICS
Catfish Clues

Catfish knew that he was different.
The other fish called him names.
He was big, and he had whiskers,
and his skin was not the same.

Schools of fish all swim together.
They all look the same.
With no teachers, math, or recess,
safety in numbers is their game.

Is that a fish? How can you tell?
Does it live in water and have scales?
Do a tail and fins help it to swim?
Do gills let it breathe oxygen?

Yes! That's a fish!

Some fish live in salty water,
oceans where they swim free.
Others live in rivers, lakes, and ponds,
or aquariums for us to see.

Fish eat what's in the water,
wherever they may live,
plants or insects, worms or frogs,
fish or shrimp, or pollywogs.

Is that a fish? How can you tell?
Does it live in water and have scales?

Do a tail and fins help it to swim?
Do gills let it breathe oxygen?

Yes! That's a fish!

Can you wiggle your tail?
Can you splash your fins?
Can you swim in the water?
Do it all again!

Can you wiggle your tail?
Can you splash your fins?
Can you swim in the water
with your fishy friends?

Catfish was a different fish.
He was happy without scales,
but just like his friends, he had fishy parts
like gills and fins and a tail.

Is that a fish? How can you tell?
Does it live in water and have scales?
Do a tail and fins help it to swim?
Do gills let it breathe oxygen?

Yes! That's a fish!

Catfish Clues

Hip Hop
Drew Temperante

Verse

1. Cat-fish knew that he was dif-ferent. The oth-er fish called him names. He was big, and he had

whisk-ers, and his skin was not the same.

Verse 2
Schools of fish all swim together.
They all look the same.
With no teachers, math, or recess,
safety in numbers is their game.

Chorus

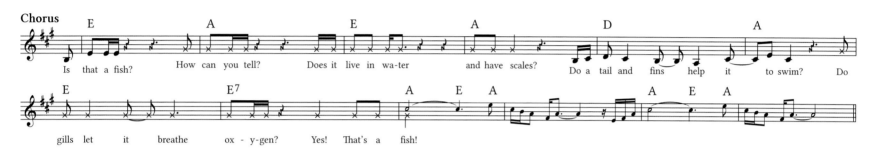

Is that a fish? How can you tell? Does it live in wa-ter and have scales? Do a tail and fins help it to swim? Do

gills let it breathe ox-y-gen? Yes! That's a fish!

Verse 3
Some fish live in salty water,
oceans where they swim free.
Others live in rivers, lakes, and ponds,
or aquariums for us to see.

Verse 4
Fish eat what's in the water,
wherever they may live,
plants or insects, worms or frogs,
fish or shrimp, or pollywogs.

Chorus

Bridge

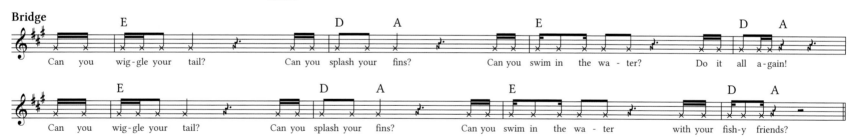

Can you wig-gle your tail? Can you splash your fins? Can you swim in the wa-ter? Do it all a-gain!

Can you wig-gle your tail? Can you splash your fins? Can you swim in the wa-ter with your fish-y friends?

Verse 5
Catfish was a different fish.
He was happy without scales,
but just like his friends, he had fishy parts
like gills and fins and a tail.

Chorus

23

GLOSSARY

aquariums—places where people can see fish and other water animals

gills—body parts on the sides of a fish; fish use their gills to breathe

oxygen—a colorless gas that people and animals need to breathe

pollywogs—young frogs; also called tadpoles

whiskers—long, stiff hairs growing on the faces and bodies of some animals

GUIDED READING ACTIVITIES

1. What did you learn about fish from reading this book? Write down three things that all fish have in common.

2. Have you ever been to or seen an aquarium? Draw one of the sea creatures you saw in the aquarium.

3. In this story, catfish learns that it is okay to be different. He has whiskers, and he doesn't have scales like other fish. How are you different from your friends and family?

TO LEARN MORE

Greve, Tom. *Freshwater Fish*. Vero Beach, FL: Rourke Publishing, 2012.

Kaspar, Anna. *What's a Fish?* New York: PowerKids Press, 2013.

Martin, Isabel. *Fish: A Question and Answer Book*. North Mankato, MN: Capstone Publishers, 2015.

Schuetz, Kari. *Fish*. Minneapolis: Bellwether Media, 2013.